DATE DUE		
NOV 29 1993		
NOV 29 1993		
11/8/94		
11-26-97		
NOV 25, 1998		

92
SQU

Jassem, Kate.

Squanto, the Pilgrim
adventure.

**LAKESHORE ELEMENTARY SCHOOL
HOLLAND, MI   49424**

SQUANTO
The Pilgrim Adventure

by Kate Jassem
illustrated by Robert Baxter

Troll Associates

Troll Associates, Mahwah, N.J.
Library of Congress Catalog Card Number: 78-18042
ISBN 0-89375-161-8

SQUANTO
The Pilgrim Adventure

Squanto raced along the sandy beach. His heart pounded. He felt the sting of broken shells cutting his feet.

He had been the first to see the white sails of the tall ship, and he wanted to be the first to bring the news to his village.

5

Everyone in the Patuxet village was busy with the day's work. The Indians' food came from the fields, forests, and lakes. All spring and summer they were busy fishing and hunting. Their catch must be dried and stored for the cold winter moons. Even the spring berries the children gathered would be dried for winter.

Now women pulled weeds in the small gardens beside each bark-covered wigwam. Small children jumped and shouted to keep birds out of the corn and beans. Several braves were fitting a long piece of birch bark over the framework of a new canoe.

Suddenly, the calm was broken as Squanto and
the other boys raced through the village, shouting, "A ship comes! White men!"

Quickly, the women took the children to hide in the deep woods. Other ships had come before. They had come in peace, but there was a great fear of the white strangers and their fire-sticks.

Squanto stood proudly beside his father. He was tall for his fourteen summers. He held his breath with excitement as the small boat came closer to shore.

"Friends!" the strangers began calling. "We are friends!"

Their leader stepped onto the beach.

"I am Captain Weymouth," he said. "You bring furs to our ship; we will give you many good things."

Squanto stared at the strange-looking men. He
could not understand why they covered themselves from head to foot when the sun was so hot.
Even their faces were covered with hair!

For many days the white men stayed to trade.
The Indians were happy with the knives, combs,
mirrors, bracelets, and rings they traded for their
furs.

11

Squanto spent most of his time with the sailors. He helped them gather firewood and find fresh water for the ship. He held his ears when they hunted with their fire-sticks.

Each day he learned their words, English words.

"We go soon," Captain Weymouth said one day. "You come with us?"

"Me?" Squanto asked.

"I will ask your father," said the Captain.

That night, Squanto's mother said nothing as she sewed new deerskin moccasins by the fire. He could see that her eyes were red and sad.

His father lit his pipe and stirred the fire. He was thinking.

"Captain Weymouth tells me he goes south with the sunrise. He wants to take you, my son. He says you will talk for him to our Indian brothers."

"Yes, Father. I want to go!"

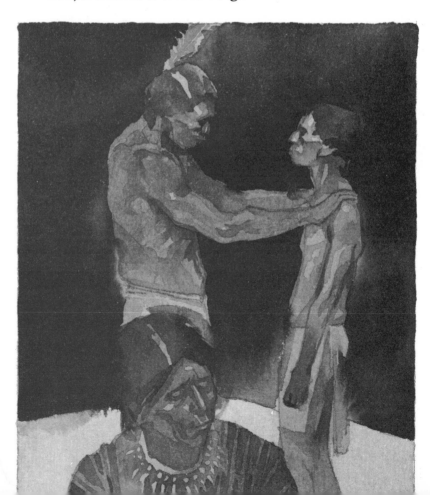

"It is good. You will help the Captain, and you will learn the white man's words and ways."

"Yes, Father. I will go!"

That night, Squanto tossed and turned on his bed of grass mats. He listened as his people sang themselves to sleep. Tomorrow night he would sleep on the tall ship!

14

With the morning tide, Squanto called his last goodbyes. The white sails filled with wind. But a sadness came upon him when he could no longer see his people on the shore.

For several weeks the boat sailed along the shoreline. It went from one village to the next, trading with the many tribes of Wampanoag Indians. Like Squanto, they spoke the Algonkian language.

Then, one morning, the ship no longer followed the rocky coast. When Squanto climbed up the tall mast, he could see no sign of land.

"We're bound for home," the sailors said.

"England, lad. We're taking you to England!"

After many weeks at sea, the ship finally reached England.

Squanto had never imagined that any place in the world could be so crowded and noisy. Side by side, like trees in the winter forest, ships of all sizes hugged the London Harbor.

As the men on board called happily to the waiting women and children below, Squanto felt a wave of loneliness. Would he ever see his own family again?

Squanto asked about everything he saw. There were so many strange things. Horses, carriages, bridges, churches, and houses, one after another. And so many people!

"Look! An Indian!" people shouted as they crowded around Squanto.

Squanto walked tall and straight. He wore feathers in his black hair, red and blue paint on his face, and a deerskin breechcloth. The hard cobblestones felt strange under his moccasins.

Squanto had left his own village thinking he would return in a few moons.

But he lived in England for nine years!

Captain Weymouth promised him that one day he would go home to his people, but one winter followed another. Now Squanto was no longer a boy. He wore English clothes and ate English food. He tried not to lose hope, but he longed to see his people.

Squanto spent much of his time near the waterfront watching the ships come and go.

One day, there was great excitement. The famous sea captain, John Smith, was signing on men to sail for the New World. He was especially looking for a young man called Squanto.

"My friend Weymouth tells me that you could be of great help to me," said Smith. "Will you come with us?"

Squanto had waited for this day for so many years!

When they finally set sail for the New World, there were two small wooden ships making the voyage. One was commanded by the red-haired Captain Smith; the other by Captain Hunt.

Squanto was glad to be on Captain Smith's ship. Among the sailors, Captain Hunt was known as a harsh and cruel man. They said he was greedy for money and cared for little else. He drove his crew without mercy.

During the long days at sea, Captain Smith talked of his great adventures in the New World. His favorite story was about a beautiful Indian princess, Pocahontas, who had saved his life.

He had sailed many seas and seen more countries than most men of his day. This was not his first crossing to the New World. In 1607, he had been with the first group of people to settle in America, in Jamestown, Virginia.

Now, Smith planned to explore the land north of Virginia. He called it New England. He asked Squanto to stay with him while he made his maps.

Each night as the sun went down, Squanto's excitement grew. He knew he was getting closer to home.

At last the day came.

"Land ho!" the sailors shouted.

On the island of Monhegan, off the coast of Maine, Squanto gave thanks to the Great Spirit.

Captain Hunt lost no time. He headed south, saying he was going to find whales.

Squanto stayed with Captain Smith. They sailed in and around the rough and rocky coast. Sometimes, they stopped at Indian villages, where the people stared at the white strangers and at the Indian who traveled with them.

24

Squanto was glad to speak again with his Indian brothers. Soon he would be with his father's people again.

It was late summer when Smith finished his maps and Squanto was free to go. He felt a great joy as he passed through the pine woods he had known as a boy. He was three days' walk from his village. But what was three days, after waiting so long?

For two days Squanto made his way south. He ate the sweet berries and nuts he found along the way.

The people in his village would be getting ready for the great Feast of the Green Corn. Every year they thanked the Great Spirit for their crops. He was thinking of the dancing and games when suddenly, a voice called out, "Squanto!"

It was Captain Hunt. He seemed to have come from nowhere! Squanto started toward him. What was the Captain doing here?

Suddenly, two sailors came from behind and threw Squanto to the ground. He struggled as they tied his hands and feet.

"Good," said the Captain. "We'll get a good price for him in Spain. Get him to the ship now."

Squanto was not the only prisoner. Captain Hunt had not caught any whales, just Indians!

With their feet and hands bound in chains, they were helpless. Squanto was sick with grief. Now he might never see his people again.

In Spain, Squanto was sold in the slave market. For several years he worked for his masters under the hot Spanish sun. His longing for home deepened, and he looked for a chance to escape.

At last he managed to get on board a boat bound for England.

But his troubles were not over. How would he get home?

He finally found a fishing boat that would sail from England to Newfoundland, in the New World. More than fourteen years had now passed since he had seen his Patuxet village.

"At least," he thought, "if I cross the ocean, I might find a way south."

In Newfoundland, Squanto had to work long, hard hours with the other sailors. They pulled nets full of fish from the cold waters until the ship's hold was full.

Squanto watched as the tall ships raced back to England to sell their catch.

Few men cared to stay in the cold, bleak North, but Squanto was used to loneliness.

29

Many months passed. When Squanto heard
about a small ship that was headed south toward
New England, he was overjoyed. As its sails bil-
lowed out against the blue sky, Squanto thought
back on all the long years of waiting and hoping.
Now, at last, he was surely going home!

Squanto's heart pounded when they reached the New England shore. He ran across the sandy beach and up the steep hillside. He could hardly breathe as he came closer to the clearing that surrounded the small village of Patuxet.

31

He stopped for a moment to listen. There was a terrible silence. Why was the field not planted? Where were the people?

Everything was deathly still.

No smoke rose from the wigwams.

No man, woman, or child was there.

Just the terrible silence.

Squanto fell to his knees and cried out to the Great Spirit.

Where were his people? Squanto had to find out what had happened to them. Why had they left their home?

He followed the worn trails in the forest until he came to the large village of Chief Massasoit.

"I am Squanto," he said to the mighty ruler of all the Wampanoag tribes. "I am of the Patuxet people."

"No more," the tall Chief said sadly. "Your people are no more. A terrible sickness has taken every member of your tribe. They have gone to the Great Spirit. You, Squanto, are the last of the Patuxet people."

Squanto walked among the people of the village. Women were grinding corn, weaving baskets, and talking together as they worked.

Young braves had returned from the forest with deer and turkeys for the autumn feasting days.

Children laughed as they played the same games Squanto had enjoyed as a boy.

For them, nothing had changed. For Squanto, nothing was the same.

For many moons, Squanto lived alone in the forest. He did not wish to see or speak to anyone. When the winter snows covered the ground, he heard the mournful cry of the wolves. His grief for his lost people was great.

Then, when the spring rains fell, a brave came to his wigwam.

"My name is Samoset," he said. "Chief Massasoit has told me of your sadness."

"The Great Spirit should have let me die across the seas," said Squanto. "My people are no more. My village is dead. I do not wish to live."

"No, Squanto. Your village is not dead! People have come from England. They have built houses there. They call your village Plymouth."

"Who told you this?" Squanto asked.

"Come. I will show you."

Samoset had learned much about the strangers. He, too, had learned to speak English. Massasoit and his people wished to trade with the new
settlers. So he asked that Samoset and Squanto
help make friends with them.

With Samoset, Massasoit, and many braves, Squanto followed the old trail to his village. There, in the clearing, he looked at the place where his people's wigwams had once stood.

Now, instead of wigwams, Squanto saw a few thatched houses. They were crudely built of sticks and mud.

Squanto walked toward the largest house. Suddenly the door opened, and men ran out with fire-sticks in their hands.

"Do not be afraid," Squanto said in English. "We come as friends."

37

Soon after, Squanto and Massasoit sat with the Pilgrim leaders—Governor John Carver, William Bradford, and Miles Standish. Squanto spoke in English, then in Algonkian, back and forth. He helped them understand each other.

"We have traveled to many lands," said the Pilgrim Fathers. "We wish only to be friends, and to worship God in our own way."

Together the leaders agreed that their people would live in peace.

Squanto could see that the settlers were thin and pale. They had little food, but they asked Massasoit and his braves to eat and drink with them.

While they were eating, the Pilgrims showed Massasoit some fine baskets they had found in the village. The baskets were full of seed corn.

Squanto could not take his eyes from the baskets. In them were the seeds grown by the hands of his own people!

"I cannot leave this place," he told Samoset. "I will stay and help these people. Like me, they are wanderers. I will show them how my people lived from the land. It is good."

Out in the bay, Squanto saw the Pilgrims' small ship, the *Mayflower*. They told him that only half the people who had crossed the ocean were still alive. So many had died during the first cruel winter.

At first they had all lived in the big Common House. Then those who were strong enough had built small one-room cabins for their families. Now, they must build more houses and store food. There was much to do.

Squanto knew he could help the Pilgrims in many ways. First, they needed to know how to find food.

It was still early spring, but Squanto showed them how to tap the maple trees for sweet sap.

Then he went down to the river with the settlers. He showed them where clams were. He stamped his feet in the mud. Fat eels came wiggling out. The Pilgrims were surprised. They had not known there was so much food nearby. The eels and clams would make good eating for the hungry people.

It was not long before the children followed Squanto everywhere.

Later, when the ground became warm, Squanto showed the Pilgrims how his father had prepared the fields for planting. It would soon be time to sow the corn.

Then Squanto put the children to work making grass nets to catch small fish in the river.

When the Pilgrims began to plant the corn, they made long, narrow rows.

"No," said Squanto. "That is not the way."

He showed them how his mother had put four seeds into a little mound of earth. He put fish around the seeds and covered them over.

"The fish will help the corn grow tall. You will see."

Squanto helped the settlers plant pumpkins, squash, and beans, too. Soon the fields were green with young leaves.

He told the children to chase the birds out of the fields, just as he had done as a child. Running and shouting was the funniest work they had ever done!

With Squanto to show them how, the men built traps and made bows and arrows. Squanto led the way through the hunting grounds he had known as a boy. Here they found deer, moose, bears, turkeys, and other wild game.

"Thanks to Squanto, we shall not go hungry this winter," they said. They were very glad for their new friend.

44

When the bright leaves began to fall, the Pilgrims harvested their crops and prepared for the long, hard winter ahead. They wanted to share their bounty with their new friends. So they asked Massasoit to bring his people for a great feast of thanksgiving.

From every house in the small village, the good smells of roasting turkeys and ducks filled the air. Squanto showed the children where to find wild nuts and bright red cranberries. Everyone had a job to do.

Chief Massasoit and some of his braves came to the feast, bringing gifts of wild turkey and deer. For several days they ate and sang side by side with the Pilgrims. The children laughed and played games with the braves. It was a good time.

On that chilly day in the fall of 1621, the Pilgrims were celebrating the first Thanksgiving Day.

Now, their storehouses were full. They were ready for the coming winter. They had made a new home where they could worship in their own way.

The Pilgrims were grateful to Massasoit and his people for their friendship in this new land.

But they gave special thanks for Squanto. For it was he who had taught them the skills they needed to survive.

Squanto stood proudly with the Pilgrims on the feasting day. For him, there had been many long, hard years. There had been unhappiness. He had lost his people. But in helping these brave settlers, he had helped himself. Now he found peace in his heart.

He was home at last!

It is believed that Squanto died about a year after this first Thanksgiving Day in the new land. But his help to the Pilgrims will long be remembered. Bradford wrote that Squanto was a special instrument sent by God for the Pilgrims' good.